Amazing
Cats

WRITTEN BY
ALEXANDRA PARSONS

PHOTOGRAPHED BY
JERRY YOUNG

Stoddart

Project editors Helen Parker and Christine Webb
Senior art editor Jacquie Gulliver
Managing editor Sophie Mitchell
Editorial director Sue Unstead
Art director Colin Walton

Special photography by Jerry Young
Illustrations by Gill Elsbury, Julie Anderson, and John Hutchinson
Animals supplied by Trevor Smith's Animal World
Editorial consultants
The staff of the Natural History Museum, London

Published in Great Britain in 1990 by Dorling Kindersley Limited
9 Henrietta Street, London, England WC2E 8PS

Published in Canada in 1990 by Stoddart Publishing Co. Limited
34 Lesmill Road, Toronto, Canada M3B 2T6

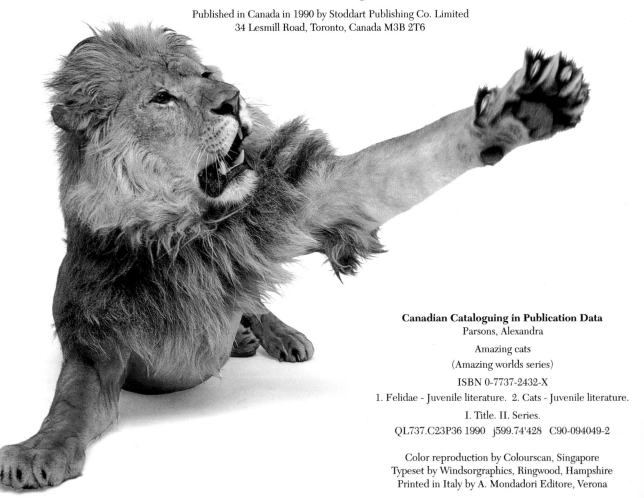

Canadian Cataloguing in Publication Data
Parsons, Alexandra

Amazing cats

(Amazing worlds series)

ISBN 0-7737-2432-X

1. Felidae - Juvenile literature. 2. Cats - Juvenile literature.

I. Title. II. Series.

QL737.C23P36 1990   j599.74'428   C90-094049-2

Color reproduction by Colourscan, Singapore
Typeset by Windsorgraphics, Ringwood, Hampshire
Printed in Italy by A. Mondadori Editore, Verona

Contents

What is a cat?

Cats are hunters that kill and eat other animals. There are three kinds of cat in the cat family tree – big cats like the lion; small cats like bobcats and house cats; and the cheetah, which is in a group by itself.

Lion

Tiger

Wildcat

Longhair   Siamese

Black panther

Ocelot   Bobcat

Cheetah

Leopard

Watch out!
All cats see well at night. By day the center of the eye, which lets in light, is narrow and slit-like; at night it is big and round.

day

night

Clever puss
Cats are known for their cleverness. In the story of Puss in Boots, a crafty cat helps his young master to marry a beautiful princess. He wins over her father, the king, with gifts of delicious food.

A good stretch

A cat's skeleton has about 40 more bones than yours, and a very flexible spine. This is why cats are so agile.

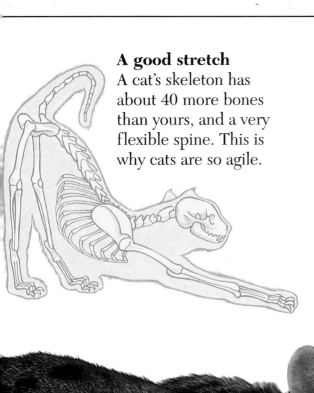

Claws in, claws out

When they're not hunting and climbing, cats pull their sharp claws into special pockets to protect them.

pulled in

pushed out

Help!

Using their sharp claws and strong legs, all cats (like this leopard cat) can climb up trees in a flash. But some pet cats have trouble climbing *down*!

This is no leopard

It has a spotted coat like a leopard's. But this leopard cat is actually a small cat that lives and hunts in the forests of Asia.

Black cat

This black tomcat spends a lot of time fighting with other male cats who stray into the area where he lives. This area is called his territory.

The pharaohs' cat

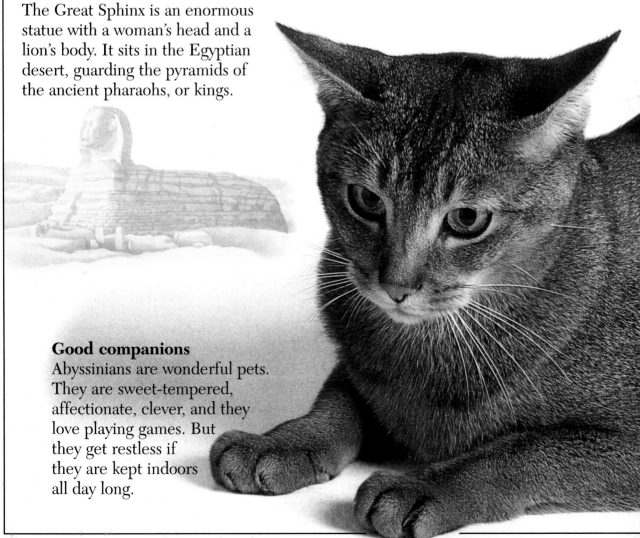

The proud-looking Abyssinian is a pet with an exotic past. It is probably related to the sacred cat of ancient Egypt, which was worshiped a long, long time ago.

A working agreement
The Egyptians pampered and protected their sacred cats. In return, the cats kept mice out of the grain stores.

Stone cat
The Great Sphinx is an enormous statue with a woman's head and a lion's body. It sits in the Egyptian desert, guarding the pyramids of the ancient pharaohs, or kings.

Good companions
Abyssinians are wonderful pets. They are sweet-tempered, affectionate, clever, and they love playing games. But they get restless if they are kept indoors all day long.

Multicolored coat

Abyssinians come in many colors. If you look closely at their fur, you will see that each hair has stripes of two or three different colors.

silver   *blue*   *normal*   *lilac*

Making music

The Abyssinian cat would be the star in any cats' choir. Its musical meow sounds more like a birdcall than a catcall.

Each hair has two or three bands of color

A good licking

Cats clean their fur with their tongues, teeth, and paws.

A long fur coat

Longhair cats may have originally come from cold countries like Russia, where their fur coats keep them warm. Their beautiful long fur needs a lot of care and attention.

Hot property
Legend says that the sacred Birman cat was found only in Burma. But one day, an American millionaire smuggled some home with him.

Wild ancestor
The house cat's wild relative, the manul (left), can hoot like an owl and yelp like a dog!

Dipped in paint
This bundle of fur is a seal colorpoint longhair. Colorpoint means that her face, ears, legs, and tail are tipped with another color, in this case a lovely warm seal brown.

Pass the hairbrush

A longhair cat needs help keeping its mop of fur clean and untangled. Just like human hair, a longhair's fur needs to be combed and brushed every day.

Handle with care

A cat likes to be picked up just so. Put one hand behind the front legs and scoop up the cat's bottom, supporting its body.

Cats turn their ears to pick up the tiniest sound

Head over heels

One sniff of a plant called catnip is enough to send cats crazy – they roll around and rub the scent of the leaves all over them.

Pardon!

Cats don't just nibble grass because it tastes good. It helps them vomit food they don't want or fur they have swallowed while grooming.

Jungle ocelot

This cat's beautiful fur is the cause of all its problems. Ocelot fur makes expensive coats, so ocelots have been hunted almost to extinction.

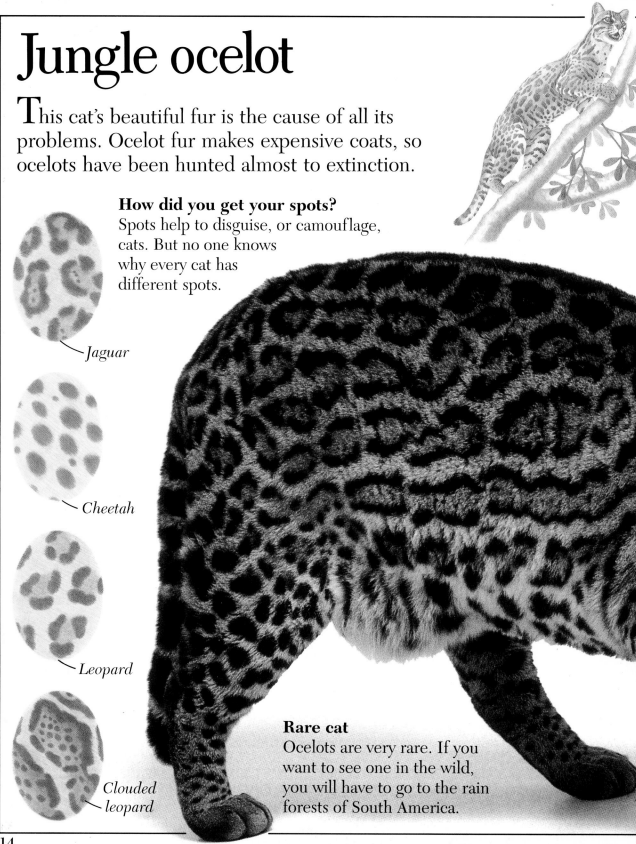

How did you get your spots?
Spots help to disguise, or camouflage, cats. But no one knows why every cat has different spots.

Jaguar

Cheetah

Leopard

Clouded leopard

Rare cat
Ocelots are very rare. If you want to see one in the wild, you will have to go to the rain forests of South America.

Sleeping platform
Ocelots are excellent climbers and can scale a tree in no time at all. Sometimes they even sleep up in the branches.

Day and night
Ocelots usually stalk their prey at night. But if the hunting is good, they will come out during the day to make the best of it.

Hard to spot
Because its fur blends in with the leafy shadows, the ocelot can sneak up on the mice and lizards that scuttle across the forest floor.

On the scent
To warn other cats to keep out of its territory, a cat sprays the boundaries with urine. It will also rub its head and feet against trees and bushes, marking them with scent from special glands.

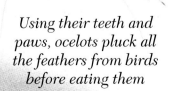

Using their teeth and paws, ocelots pluck all the feathers from birds before eating them

Bobcat

This little wildcat lives in forests and deserts. In the summer, its coat is brown. But when the snows come, the coat grows longer and turns grayish-white.

Baby den
Baby bobcats, or kits, are born in a den. The mother usually has two kits in each litter.

Bobtail
The bobcat is a kind of lynx. Lynxes have spotted fur, pointed ears, and little beards, or ruffs. The bobcat gets its name from its short, stubby bobtail.

Cats feel their way with the help of their whiskers

Here, there, and everywhere
North America is the bobcat's home. It lives in many different places: from the hot, dry deserts of Mexico to the cold, snowy mountains of Canada and the marshy swamps of Florida.

The goddess Venus and the cat

Venus once changed a cat into a woman so that she could marry a handsome man. But when she spotted a mouse, the poor woman couldn't resist chasing it. Immediately, she became a cat again.

Forest hunter

Bobcats hunt at night, creeping up and pouncing with a huge bound on rabbits, birds, and small deer.

Glowing eyes

Have you seen a cat's eyes glowing in the dark? They glow because a special layer inside the eye, the tapetum, bounces light back like a mirror.

large back feet for walking in the snow

Hide-and-seek

The bobcat often lives near towns. It is so swift and quiet that most people don't know when there's a bobcat around.

King of beasts

Lions are huge and powerful wild cats. They don't meow like pet cats. Lions have special voice boxes so they can roar very loudly and deeply to scare enemies.

Family life
Lions live on the hot, grassy plains of Africa in groups called prides. They are the only cats that live together like a family.

Hunting tools
Lions can see, smell, and hear better than humans. They also have powerful jaws and strong, sharp teeth for slicing through meat.

Lady killers
Female lions, or lionesses, are smaller than males. They bring up the cubs and do most of the hunting. Quietly they charge, knock the animal to the ground, and kill it quickly with a bite to the throat.

The whip hand
Lions are not easy to tame, but people have been keeping them for hundreds of years.

First pickings
Although the lioness catches the food, the male lion has first pickings. When he has had his fill, the rest of the family can then join in.

A good turn

A slave boy called Androcles once helped a wild lion by pulling a thorn out of its paw. Soon after, he was captured by the Romans and thrown to the lions. But he was saved by one of the lions – the same one he had helped before.

Defending the family

Male lions have large, thick manes of hair which make them look even bigger and fiercer. Their main job is to defend the pride and its territory.

The lion's sharp claws can be pulled in

19

Spot the leopard

When they're not out hunting, these strong and graceful cats spend a lot of time lazing around in trees. Sadly, many leopards are killed each year for their beautiful spotted fur.

Nursery school
Leopard cubs stay with their mother until they are between one and two years old. They learn how to hunt and kill.

Spotted friend
In many ancient legends and paintings, leopards were used as a sign of strength and beauty. Bacchus, the Greek god of wine, was often shown with one of these beautiful and powerful creatures at his side.

The leopard's spotted fur enables it to hide in the jungles of Africa and Asia

Cloud cover

Clouded leopards are different from other leopards. They are smaller, and the bigger markings on their fur look more like clouds than spots. They have long tails and are good climbers.

Big cat

The leopard below is 18 years old – quite old for a leopard – but he still enjoys a playful roll on his back.

Ssshh!

Leopards hunt alone, usually at night. They wait silently, sometimes in a tree, ready to pounce on a passing meal.

Leopard larder

Leopards often drag their "kill" up into a tree, so they can eat slowly, without having to share it.

Like most cats, leopards can push out their claws for hunting and climbing

A cat that swims?

Most pet cats hate water and will scratch and hiss rather than get wet. But this pet cat from Turkey loves to swim, especially in warm, shallow streams or pools.

The fur is smooth, silky, and slightly oily to make it more waterproof

No vest
The Turkish swimming cat has no woolly undercoat like other longhaired cats. This means that its wet fur dries out much more quickly.

Holy cat
The Turkish swimming cat has a white patch on its forehead. Turkish people used to believe that this mark was the thumbprint of their god, Allah.

Gone fishing

Many wild cats think nothing of getting wet if it means they can catch a tasty fish or frog. This fishing cat from China has special webbed paws for swimming.

Cold comfort

These cats come from Lake Van in the Turkish mountains. In winter their coats grow longer to keep them warm in the bitterly cold weather.

Summer wardrobe

Turkish swimming cats lose their long fur coats in the hot Turkish summer. This is called molting.

Most Turkish swimming cats have pale amber eyes

A wet, pink nose is the sign of a healthy cat

Traveling cats

Sailors used to think that a black cat on board ship brought them good luck. It certainly kept away the rats!

Desert caracal

This fierce-looking cat comes from the deserts of Africa and Asia. It has short fur to help it keep cool, and it can go for a long time without water.

Desert stalker
The caracal does most of its hunting at night. It has to be very fast to catch its prey of hares, birds, lizards, and small antelope.

Dinner flies past
Caracals are so good at jumping that they can catch a bird as it takes off. In India, contests are held with tame caracals to see which can strike down the most pigeons in one leap.

Help with the hunt
A long time ago, in India, people trained caracals to catch gazelles and birds for them.

Standing snack
Sometimes a caracal will stand up on its hind legs to eat – not like a cat at all.

The word caracal means "black ears" in Turkish

The sand cat
The sand cat (above) has mats of hair under its paws to protect it from the burning rocks and sand.

Born blind
Like most kittens, baby caracals are born with their eyes closed.

Paws for thought
Cats have five toes on their front feet. But the fifth toe doesn't touch the ground, so it leaves no mark.

front paw print

fifth toe

claws in

claws out

Forest wildcat

Wildcats may look like pet tabby cats – but they're not. They are ferocious, powerful, and hard to tame. They live in thick forests and on craggy mountains – far away from people.

All alone
The wildcat guards its own special hunting area. It has its own tracks and paths, safe places to sleep, and favorite claw-sharpening trees. It won't let any other wildcat hunt there.

Fierce kittens
Female wildcats give birth to four or five kittens. At first the kittens look cute and playful, but at three months they are snarling just like their parents.

Charming!
When a wildcat is angry, it flattens its ears and curls back its lips to show its long, sharp front teeth.

Wildcat strike

A sudden strike in a factory is sometimes called a wildcat strike.

Keep your fur on!
When a cat is scared, it arches its back and lowers its tail, and all the hairs on its body stand on end.

The wild cat's markings make it hard to see in the forest

Gone fishing
Like many house cats, wild cats love fish. They will sometimes spend hours going in and out of the water to catch them.

Shadowy figures
One kind of wild cat lives in the forests and highlands of Scotland. During the day it sleeps in dens among the rocks and trees. When it slips out at night to hunt, it keeps to the shadows.

Nine lives

Cats are agile and fast, and always seem to land on their feet when they're in a tight spot. They can jump a gap twice the length of their body with no trouble at all. They are such survivors that people often say they have nine lives.

On the prowl
Like all cats, this ginger tom walks on "tiptoe." Its body is stretched out and close to the ground, ready to leap or pounce at a moment's notice.

Cats are such good balancers, that they can walk along a strip of wood as narrow as a tightrope

The great leap
Cats move just like ballet dancers. They even jump gracefully. With a huge push from the back legs, this cat launches into the air. Using its tail for balance, it stretches toward the ground, and touches down with its front legs first.

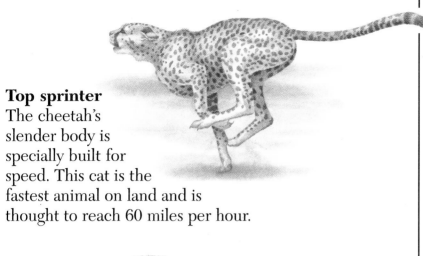

Top sprinter
The cheetah's slender body is specially built for speed. This cat is the fastest animal on land and is thought to reach 60 miles per hour.

Practice makes perfect
Catching dinner isn't as easy as it looks. Cats have to be strong, alert, and very swift. Even pet cats spend a lot of time learning to stalk and kill mice and birds.

Cat burglars
Some thieves are nimble – good at scaling walls, squeezing into tiny gaps, and then making a quick getaway. That's why they are called cat burglars, after some of the best climbers around.

Index